D1425950

A SPOTTER'S GUIDE

Film ^and TV Locations

Scout out the world's top spots for famous film and TV scenes

Ladies and gentlemen, welcome to the ultimate movie book.

The movies take you places: cinema is a mode of transport. In just 90 minutes, you can be whisked all the way around the globe – perhaps with a dotted red line marking your progress on a map as you go. Some films take you even farther, out of this world and to other galaxies far, far away. As Roman Polanski put it, a film hasn't done its job correctly unless you forgot you were sitting in a theatre.

What's great is that the converse is often true: there are some places that can transport you into the world of a movie. If you want to feel like James Bond, try going to James Bond Island (page 10). In a Holly Golightly mood? Have a danish pastry and some coffee outside Tiffany's in Manhattan (page 62). Or want to feel like Rocky? Then run up the steps to the Philadelphia Museum (page 24) and put your hands in the air like a champ when you get to the top.

This book is about the real-world places that provided the backdrops and settings for some of our most memorable collective dreams. Some of these locations played themselves and others were dressed up to look like somewhere else. But they all added texture and colour and weight to the visions of our best TV- and film-makers.

Who needs CGI when the real world looks as fabulous and varied as this?

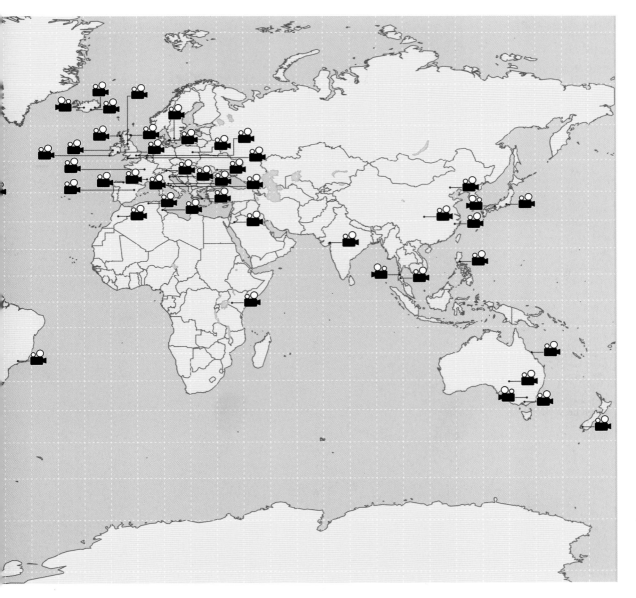

The Martian

2015

Wadi Rum, Jordan

Despite the support and involvement of NASA, it wasn't practical for Ridley Scott to shoot pro-science Robinson Crusoe story *The Martian* on Mars, so he returned to the next best thing: Wadi Rum in Jordan, where he'd also shot scenes set on an alien planet in *Prometheus* (2012).

Wadi Rum is also known as 'the Valley of the Moon' but 'the Valley of Mars' might be more apt. *Red Planet* (2000) and the *Last Days on Mars* (2013) were both filmed there, too. As were key scenes in *Lawrence of Arabia* (1962).

©JOE WINDSOR-WILLIAMS/LONELY PLANET

©MARTIN BISOF/500PX

The Motorcycle Diaries

2004

Machu Picchu, Peru

In 1952, during a year-long road trip through South America on a Norton motorcycle, the 23-year-old medical student and future revolutionary Ernesto 'Che' Guevara had a political awakening. In Walter Salles's beautifully photographed movie version of events, young Che is profoundly moved by the 15th-century Incan mountaintop city of Machu Picchu, and wonders aloud about the progressive utopia South America might have become if not for the Spanish conquistadors. Human sacrifices notwithstanding.

©JDONOVAN REESE/GETTY IMAGES

RoboCop

1988

Dallas City Hall, Texas, USA

The great cyberpunk sci-fi cinema of the 1980s envisaged dehumanised, depersonalised worlds. For example, *RoboCop* took IM Pei's design for Dallas City Hall, a bold modernist inverted pyramid he intended 'to convey an image of the people', and turned it into the headquarters of OCP, the ruthless and unfeeling private corporation that supplies law enforcement in a dystopian future. Still, cool robots!

Roman Holiday

1953

Santa Maria in Cosmedin, Rome, Italy

Legend has it that the Bocca della Verità – an ancient Roman marble manhole cover which is now in the portico of the church of Santa Maria in Cosmedin – acts like a kind of primitive lie detector. It's probably nonsense. But it is true that you can pinpoint the exact moment that the world fell in love with Audrey Hepburn to the supposedly unscripted bit in *Roman Holiday* when she reacts to Gregory Peck sticking his hand in its mouth.

© JAMES HARDY/GETTY IMAGES

FRÉDÉRIC LEGRAND - COMEO/SHUTTERSTOCK.COM

Marie Antoinette

2006

Palace of Versailles, France

Perhaps because she intended a more sympathetic portrait of the cake-eating queen than most, or perhaps simply because she films beautiful things so beautifully, Sofia Coppola was given the keys to the castle: that is, unprecedented access to any of the Palace of Versailles's 700 rooms that she wished to film in.

The Man With the Golden Gun

1974

James Bond Island (Khao Phing Kan), Thailand

Khao Phing Kan rarely goes by its given name, and has been locally known as James Bond Island ever since Christopher Lee's supervillain Scaramanga hid his 'solex agitator' in the limestone karst tower off its shore. Why Scaramanga also built a funhouse and hall of mirrors on the island is anyone's guess, but it's best not to question the logic of the Roger Moore–era Bond films too closely.

©MUSTANG_79/GETTY IMAGES/ISTOCKPHOTO

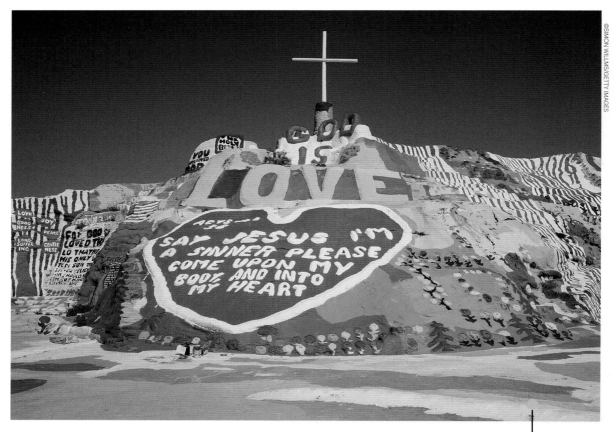

©SIMON WILLMS/GETTY IMAGES

Into the Wild

2007
Salvation Mountain, Colorado Desert, California, USA

Christopher McCandless was a young man who rechristened himself Alexander Supertramp and went a-wandering in the American wilderness in search off Huck Finn–type adventures and Thoreauvian transcendental experience. Leonard Knight was an outsider artist who spent the last 30 years of his life on the creation of a painted mountain emblazoned with messages about God, love and salvation. It makes total sense that the latter would feature in Sean Penn's heartfelt biographical film about the former.

©MALYN/500PX

The Lost Boys

1987

Santa Cruz Boardwalk, California, USA

With all those flashing lights and thrill-seekers, all that motion and excitement, is it any wonder that a small-town Californian boardwalk after dark might act as a beacon for young men with motorbikes and leather jackets, punky haircuts, pointy teeth and lots of rock-and-roll, stay-up-all-night attitude.

It's not a major cause for alarm, unless it seems like your older brother has become one of them. Or like Mom might find out.

The Shining

1980

Timberline Lodge, Mount Hood, Oregon, USA

Here is the exterior of the Overlook, the hotel in which winter caretaker Jack Torrence loses his mind in one of the most remarkable horror movies ever made. Sadly if you visit, you won't get to see the '70s patterned carpets that are the scariest thing in the film, as the interior scenes were shot on enormous, exquisitely detailed sets built in Elstree studios in the UK.

© DON LOWE/GETTY IMAGES

©NOVARC IMAGES/ALAMY

The Lives of Others

2006
Berlin-Hohenschönhausen Memorial, Berlin, Germany

Although it didn't officially exist, Hohenschönhausen prison is where the Stasi did its interrogating, torturing and imprisoning of East German citizens during the period depicted in Florian Henckel von Donnersmarck's evocative political thriller *The Lives of Others*. Scenes were set here but the interiors were shot in a film studio.

Now home to a museum, it's a memorial to the era and a powerful reminder of the horrors that can result from the combination of political paranoia and state surveillance. As is the film.

©ALVARO MINGUITO/500PX

Pan's Labyrinth

2006
Belchite, Zaragoza, Spain

Guillermo del Toro's dark fairytale, about a girl who enters a fantasy world to escape the reality of life as the new stepdaughter of a fascist army officer after the Spanish Civil War, is full of strange sights and special effects. But this place, where her journey between worlds begins, is real: the ruins of an entire town that was destroyed by the war, then left by Franco as a symbol of his victory, and eventually reclaimed as a memorial to the dead.

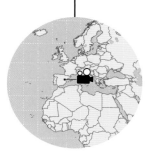

©LEN SALTIEL/500PX

Brokeback Mountain

2005

Kananaskis Country, Alberta, Canada

Not many films have a better feel for a place, or for how a landscape can dramatically sculpt the lives of the people living in it, than *Brokeback Mountain* has for the small towns and the rugged countryside of 1960s and 1970s Wyoming. And this is despite the fact that the film was shot 965km further up the Rocky mountain range, in Alberta, Canada.

©LOU JONES/GETTY IMAGES

Jaws

1975

Martha's Vineyard, Massachusetts, USA

Derr-derr … Derr-derr … Der-der der-der … Der-der-der-der-der-der-de-de-de-de …

In 1975, the swanky Cape Cod island resort Martha's Vineyard played Amity Island: a beach community that was terrorised by a big, mean great white shark that developed a taste for tender young human flesh, could chew its way through the hull of a fishing boat, and had its own ominous theme tune. And to this day, people are scared to go in the water.

©JOHN HARPER/GETTY IMAGES

Vicky Cristina Barcelona

2008

Oviedo, Spain

Rarely was a film director more associated with one place than Woody Allen was with New York. But that was before he began to get overseas funding on the condition that he shoot abroad, and we got films such as *Vicky Cristina Barcelona*, a charming and sexy romantic drama about a *ménage à quatre*, with picture-postcard views of Barcelona and Oviedo that make them look like the kind of places where cares and inhibitions just melt away.

©YUSUN CHUNG/500PX

Gattaca

1997

Marin County Civic Center, California, USA

Thanks to his utopian, Usonian vision for modern living, and the cantilevering and clean lines of his designs, Frank Lloyd Wright's buildings continue to look like they could only exist in a space-age future, along with jetpacks and monorails. You don't expect to find them in the real world, but it's no surprise that they turn up in sci-fi films constantly. Marin County Civic Center doubled as the underground compound in George Lucas's *THX-1138* as well as acting as the headquarters of the sinister Gattaca Aerospace Corporation.

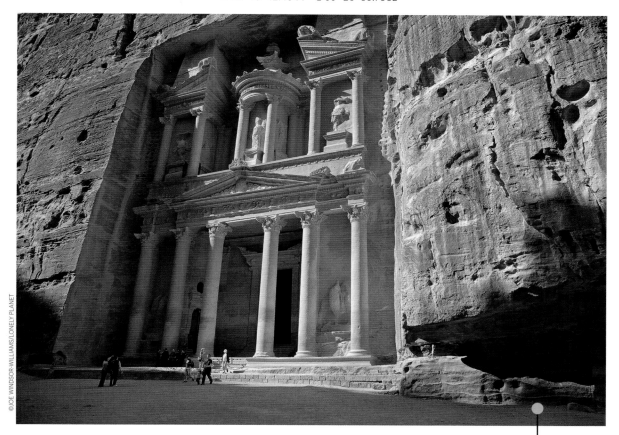

©JOE WINDSOR-WILLIAMS/LONELY PLANET

Indiana Jones and the Last Crusade

1989

Al-Khazneh, Petra, Jordan

If you were the world's greatest archaeologist-adventurer taking your dad along on a quest to find the Holy Grail, where might you look? A good starting place would be Petra in Jordan, the 2300-year-old city described in a sonnet by John William Burgon: 'From the rock as if by magic grown / eternal, silent, beautiful alone! … a rose-red city half as old as time.'

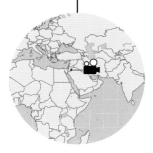

©JOHN AND TINA REID/GETTY IMAGES

Game of Thrones

2011–

Dubrovnik, Croatia

Dubrovnik is a city that some archaeologists date to before the common era, while the fortifications and city wall that encircle it are from the Middle Ages. It has variously been called the Croatian Athens and the Pearl of the Adriatic, but it will be a long time before people stop thinking of it as King's Landing, Westeros, capital of the Seven Kingdoms.

©SAMUEL BORGES PHOTOGRAPHY/SHUTTERSTOCK

Rocky

1976

**Philadelphia
Art Museum,
Pennsylvania, USA**

The Philadelphia Museum of Art houses more than quarter of a million objects. It receives in excess of half a million visitors a year – though many of them come for its most culturally significant artefact, which lies outside the main gallery. The 72 steps leading to its entrance are popularly known as the Rocky Steps, after their appearance in cinema's most famous and inspiring training montage. Local legend has it that it is impossible to climb them without 'Gonna Fly Now', the theme from *Rocky*, playing in your head.

© J MICHAEL ROBERTS/GETTY IMAGES

An American Werewolf in London

1981

Black Mountains, Wales

This green and pleasant bit of rolling countryside looks like a nice place for a stroll, doesn't it? Not at all the sort of place where you'd have to be warned about straying from the path. And yet it stood in for the Yorkshire moors in John Landis's howlingly funny horror-comedy, in which 1980s Britain was made to seem like a very strange and foreboding place, where even a friendly rural pub like the Slaughtered Lamb has a pentagram on the wall.

Dirty Dancing

1987

**Firefly Cove,
Lake Lure,
North Carolina, USA**

'You know, the best place to practise lifts is in the water,' says Johnny Castle, the smouldering holiday-camp dance instructor who shows teenager Francis 'Baby' Houseman the time of her life one summer at camp in the early 1960s. And this is the picturesque lake that he takes her to, where they get all wet and giggly practising one of modern cinema's most famous dance moves.

©ALEX GRICHENKO/GETTY IMAGES

© IVAN VDOVIN/GETTY IMAGES

Pride and Prejudice

2005

Chatsworth House, Derbyshire, UK

Some Jane Austen scholars believe the author had the 16th-century stately home Chatsworth in mind when describing Mr Darcy's Pemberley estate: 'A large, handsome, stone building, standing well on rising ground.' And even if Chatsworth wasn't Austen's Pemberley, it is for anyone whose favourite *Pride and Prejudice* adaptation is the 2005 one with Keira Knightley.

©ULLSTEIN BILD/CONTRIBUTOR/GETTY IMAGES

Interstellar

2014
Svínafellsjökull glacier, Vatnajökull National Park, Iceland

In Christopher Nolan's grand sci-fi epic, humanity's last hopes of effecting an escape from its dying home planet lie on the other side of a wormhole near Saturn, where a planet made entirely of frozen clouds is about as hospitable as things get. 'Cold, stark but undeniably beautiful,' is how they describe the landscape in the movie, a description that also applies to the glacier where it was filmed.

©ANDREW MONTGOMERY/LONELY PLANET

Chitty Chitty Bang Bang

1968

Neuschwanstein Castle, Bavaria, Germany

Ludwig II of Bavaria's romanesque-revival hilltop castle could hardly look more like the home of a fairytale princess if it was painted pink and had the Disney logo suspended above it. Indeed, it was the model for Sleeping Beauty's castle in both Disney's 1959 film and his Californian theme park.

But film-loving children probably know it best as the home of Baron Bomburst, ruler of Vulgaria. Whether or not this was intended as a slight on Ludwig and Walt's taste in castles, movie history does not record.

©CHRISTOPHE SIMON/STAFF/GETTY IMAGES

City of God

2003

Favelas of Rio de Janeiro, Brazil

Fernando Meirelles's tense gangster drama doesn't make you want to visit the favelas of Rio, exactly, so much as it makes you thank the heavens you weren't born into the same cycles of poverty and violence as its characters. But rarely has a film captured the distinctive energy and the life of a city so well. And there isn't a film with a funkier samba soundtrack to be found anywhere.

©VISTAS FROM SONI RAKESH/GETTY IMAGES

Slumdog Millionaire

2008
Chhatrapati Shivaji Terminus, Mumbai

Completed in 1887, this gothic-revival architectural wonder and Unesco world heritage site is a Mumbai landmark, and an obvious location choice for two key scenes in Danny Boyle's masala melodrama: a colourful and kinetic picaresque about abject poverty, which would have seemed a lot less feel-good without the climactic song and dance routine on platform four.

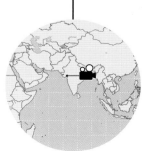

©MELODIOUS VISION/GETTY IMAGES

The Last Emperor

1987

The Forbidden City, Beijing, China

One of the wonderful things about the movies is that they transport you to places you never thought you'd see. For example, the former imperial palace in China isn't called the Forbidden City for nothing, and Bernardo Bertolucci's ravishing historical epic about its final resident was the first western film granted permission to film there.

©DANITA DELIMONT/GETTY IMAGES

Manhattan

1979

**Sutton Place Park,
Manhattan, USA**

Spend the night walking and talking with a beautiful writer, and end up on this bench at 5am watching the dawn light spread across the East River and illuminate the Queensboro Bridge. Imagine the same scene with black-and-white cinematography by Gordon Willis, and Gershwin playing in the background… congratulations, you've just recreated an iconic scene fit for a movie poster.

©YURY PROKOPENKO/GETTY IMAGES

Mad Max 2

1981

Silverton, New South Wales, Australia

Welcome to Silverton, population as of the last census: 89. Either there's something about the light here, or it looks like the very definition of a typical outback township, because films including *The Adventures of Priscilla, Queen of the Desert* (1994), *Wake in Fright* (1971) and *Mad Max 2* were all shot in and around it.

Mind you, *Mad Max 2* is set in a 'maelstrom of decay in which ordinary men were battered and mashed', so think twice before you visit.

©CULTURA RM EXCLUSIVE/BEN PIPE PHOTOGRAPHY/GETTY IMAGES

Ghostbusters

1984

New York Public Library, NY, USA

In 1984, the reading room of the New York Public Library became internationally famous as the site of the first encounter between a ghost and the disgraced academics and parapyschology researchers who came to be known as the Ghostbusters. It was not an auspicious first meeting, yet the 'busters went on to save the world shortly after, by closing the gates to hell.

©ALEXANDER SPATARI/GETTY IMAGES

The Bourne Identity

2002

Little Venice, Mikonos, Greece

The adventures of the American amnesiac superspy Jason Bourne are a riposte to the glossy travel-brochure aesthetic and post–British Empire wish-fulfilment of James Bond's adventures. Hence the shared initials. So although he's chased all over the globe, Bourne rarely gets a chance to take in any sights. It isn't until the very end of his first film that he gets a moment's peace, and can have a think about hiring a scooter and taking a look around Mikonos.

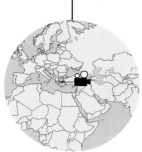

©ANDERS EKHOLM/GETTY IMAGES

The Seventh Seal

1957

**Hovs Hallar,
Skåne, Sweden**

Look at this beach scene: quite pretty, huh? No doubt some people might even see in it the glory of God's creation. Not Ingmar Bergman, though. He sees the perfect spot for a nice game of chess with the sardonic figure of Death in an existential drama about the search for meaning in a godless universe.

Gladiator

2000

Aït Benhaddou, Morocco

Swords and sandals at the ready…Aït Benhaddou is a deserted fortified city along the former caravan route between the Sahara and Marrakesh, which has provided a backdrop for films such as *The Man Who Would Be King*, *The Last Temptation of Christ*, *Kundun*, *The Mummy* and *Gladiator*. The coliseum set on which said gladiator did battle is still standing in Atlas Studios, the world's largest film studio complex, in nearby Ouarzazate.

©PATRICIA HOFMEESTER/500PX

©4NADIA/GETTY IMAGES

The Goonies

1985
Astoria, Oregon, USA

Come to Astoria, the first permanent settlement on the Pacific coast of the United States; home of the fictional Goon Docks; birthplace of the truffle shuffle. If you follow the right map, you might even find some buried pirate treasure.

If you come on 7 June, you'll find the town celebrating what it has declared Offical Goonies Day. *Short Circuit*, *Kindergarten Cop* and *Free Willy* were all filmed hereabouts as well, but they don't get their own day.

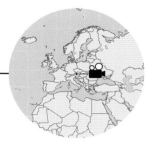

©MARCO WONG/GETTY IMAGES/MOMENT RF

The Sound of Music

1965

Salzkammergut, Austria

This is not just any chocolate-box pretty scene. These are the hills that are famously alive with the sound of music. You should climb every one of them, and ford every stream – this land represents life, freedom and glorious possibility.

©EMYU/GETTY IMAGES

Easy Rider

1969

Route 66, USA

While it's true that much of it has been rerouted or decommissioned, the mythology of Route 66 remains. At the RoadHouse Bar & Grill, west of Flagstaff in Arizona, the No Vacancies sign from the featured motel is displayed above the bar. Grab your gold football helmet and get your kicks on what's left of Route 66, with the ghosts of Captain America and Billy riding by your side: two wide-eyed longhairs on a journey to discover America and the freedom of the open road.

©DAN HUNTLEY PHOTOGRAPHY/GETTY IMAGES/FLICKR RF

La Dolce Vita

1960
Trevi fountain, Rome, Italy

This 50m-wide 18th-century baroque marvel was already *numero uno* among Rome's 2000-odd fountains before the Swedish sex symbol Anita Ekberg clambered in for a cheeky midnight dip in the most *célèbre* scene in Federico Fellini's Palme d'Or-winning *cause célèbre*.

Now, the Trevi is forever associated with everything that is glamorous, carefree and appealing about *la dolce vita*.

©MINE BEYAZ/GETTY IMAGES

Anchorman: The Legend of Ron Burgundy

2004

Long Beach, California, USA

'It was discovered by the Germans in 1904,' says 1970s local newsreader Ron Burgundy as he surveys the city in which he lives and serves. 'They named it San Diego, which of course in German means: "A Whale's Vagina."' But then, Ron Burgundy is a buffoon. He also thinks that diversity is an old, old wooden ship that was used during the Civil War era.

And as it happens, almost all the exterior scenes in *Anchorman* were filmed 193km north, in Long Beach.

©JOHN HARPER/GETTY IMAGES

The Beach

2000

Ko Phi Phi Lee, Thailand

Alex Garland's 1996 novel *The Beach* is about backpacker culture, and the quixotic search for unspoiled territory away from the paths already beaten by tourists. Putting aside for a moment the fact that it all turns a bit *Lord of the Flies* towards the end, Danny Boyle's adaptation really does make this Thai island look like some kind of 21st-century Eden.

©AMAR GROVER/GETTY IMAGES

Star Wars

1977

**Hotel Sidi Driss,
Matmâta, Tunisia**

Luke Skywalker once dismissed his uncle's homestead – in fact the whole of their home planet of Tatooine – as the point farthest from the centre of the universe, and he said he couldn't wait to leave.

The familiar-looking ancient Berber cave dwellings in Matmâta, on the other hand, on the northern fringe of the Sahara desert, still strike most of us as extremely exotic and cool, and people will travel miles to see them.

©MATTHEW LLOYD/GETTY IMAGES

Downton Abbey

2010–15

Highclere Castle, Hampshire, England

Part of the appeal of Downton Abbey lies in its nostalgic celebration of a vanished era of deference and rigid social order in which, whether aristocrat or servant, everyone at least knew their place.

That's the theory anyway. It's worth remembering that the British aristocracy hasn't gone anywhere, and although you can visit the vast 17th-century stately home that played Downton Abbey on certain days of the year, it still belongs to the Earl of Carnarvon.

Neighbours

1985–
Pin Oak Court, Melbourne, Australia

Ah, Ramsey Street, Erinsborough, the most familiar, most instantly recognisable suburban cul-de-sac in Australia, where the sun is always shining, a friendly cricket match is eternally in progress and, with a little understanding, good neighbours will always become good friends.

©COASTER/ALAMY STOCK PHOTO

©JSGOODWIN4813/GETTY IMAGES

Moonrise Kingdom

2012

Conanicut Island Light, Rhode Island, New England, USA

Nothing gets to be in a film by US indie cinema's most impeccable visual stylist, Wes Anderson, without it looking like it has been lifted from the pages of an exquisitely pretty picture book. A case in point, this 1886 lighthouse, the home of one of the precocious 12-year-old runaways in Anderson's droll paean to lovers-on-the-run movies, and to the magic and romance of childhood summer adventures.

©RYAN PYLE/CONTRIBUTOR/GETTY IMAGES

N 64° 4' 26.4864'' W 16° 13' 10.9848''

Die Another Day

2002
Jökulsárlón, Iceland

An adventure destination of choice for the movies' most action-loving types, the glacial lake Jökulsárlón is where Bruce Wayne goes for his ninja training in *Batman Begins* and where James Bond goes skiing in *A View to a Kill*. It stood in for Siberia in *Lara Croft: Tomb Raider* and, perhaps most memorably, it's where the villain built his ice palace and Bond gets into a chase in an invisible car in *Die Another Day*.

©STEVE SNOWDEN/GETTY IMAGES

Breaking Bad

2008–13

Twisters, 4257 Isleta Blvd, Albuquerque, New Mexico, USA

This branch of the 20-outlet New Mexican fast-food chain Twisters – despite it being a four-time winner of *Albuquerque Magazine's* 'Best of the City' Best Burrito award – arguably doesn't look like much. But then, nor should an establishment one wants to use as a front for a methamphetamine dealing business, so it makes sense that this Twisters was used as the location for the flagship branch of Los Pollos Hermanos. Where something delicious is always cooking.

©LAURENCE PHELAN

Twin Peaks

1990-

Twede's Cafe, North Bend, Washington, USA

Nestled amid the Douglas fir trees in America's Pacific Northwest, the small north Washington border town of Twin Peaks is such an odd little out-of-time, between-worlds kind of place – 'a place both wonderful and strange' – that it almost comes as a surprise that you can visit real-world locations such as the diner that doubled as the Double-R diner. It's said that they do a damn fine coffee and cherry pie.

Wild

2014

Pacific Northwest Trail, USA

There's nothing like a 1770km hike through much of North America's most challenging wilderness and most awe-inspiring scenery to put your human-scale problems into perspective. That's certainly what Cheryl Strayed found, and the 2014 film adaptation of her literary memoir and travelogue, *Wild,* has much the same effect.

© GREG VAUGHN/GETTY IMAGES

©TERRY WILSON/GETTY IMAGES

Star Trek

1966–69
Vasquez Rocks
Natural Area Park,
California, USA

It's funny how often the final frontier turns out to have been a mere 48km north of Hollywood.

The desert area featuring this particular sandstone formation has featured in countless films and TV shows. Mostly westerns (from *The Lone Ranger* to *Blazing Saddles*) and sci-fi (from *Power Rangers Turbo* to *Amazon Women on the Moon*). But the area will always be known as Kirk's Rock, thanks to William Shatner's Captain Kirk being beamed there for a fight with a stuntman in a rubber alien costume.

©DENNIS K JOHNSON/GETTY IMAGES

Breakfast at Tiffany's

1961

**Tiffany & Co,
New York**

Charles Tiffany & Co's 'fancy goods emporium' had been selling high-class merchandise since 1837. Then Audrey Hepburn's effortlessly glamorous good-time girl Holly Golightly takes a wistful look through its windows in the early hours of one morning, and all of a sudden the place is globally famous and synonymous with romance, diamond rings, and everything a young woman attempting to make it in mid-century Manhattan is supposed to desire.

©ADELA LOCONTE / CONTRIBUTOR/GETTY IMAGES

Birdman

2014

**St James Theatre,
Broadway, New York**

Golden-age Hollywood cinema was full of films about Broadway, which, after all, is where it found so many of its early stars and stories. But golden-age Hollywood movies were all filmed on sets, so if you want to experience the bustle and practically smell the greasepaint of the real Broadway in a movie, watch Alejandro González Iñárritu's exhilarating one-take backstage drama *Birdman*.

Lord of the Rings: The Fellowship of the Ring

2001

Fiordland National Park, New Zealand

Part of the success of Peter Jackson's adaptations of JRR Tolkein's fantasy novels is that computers were finally up to the task of digitally rendering Middle Earth in all its splendour. And part of their success is that they were filmed in locations so beautiful as to look like they've been digitally generated.

Can you tell, for example, if this is a CGI fantasyland just south of the elven town of Rivendell, or just what New Zealand looks like?

©DAVID RIVEST/500PX

©JUSTIN FOULKES/LONELY PLANET

Way of the Dragon

1972

The Coliseum, Rome, Italy

In 1972, Bruce Lee was making his first film as writer, director and star, while Chuck Norris was making his movie debut. But they were clearly destined to become two colossi of martial arts cinema, so where else but the Coliseum in Rome would make a befitting backdrop for the exquisitely choreographed climactic showdown between them?

©GEORGE CLERK/GETTY IMAGES

The Third Man

1949

**Wiener Riesenrad,
Prater amusement
park, Vienna, Austria**

Talk about dizzying heights...
This 64m-tall, 119-year-old
Viennese landmark is where
Orson Welles delivers his
famous speech insulting
the Swiss in the most
memorable scene in Carol
Reed's peerless Graham
Greene adaptation *The
Third Man*. It's also where

Jesse and Céline have their
first kiss in *Before Sunrise*,
a lovely paean to the
romance of foreign travel
and the beginning of one of
modern cinemas's greatest
love stories.

©MARTIN CHARLES HATCH/SHUTTERSTOCK

Betty Blue

1986

Gruissan Plage, Languedoc, France

One of the key films of French cinema's stylish 'cinéma du look' movement of the 1980s, Jean-Jacques Beineix's steamy romantic melodrama *Betty Blue* made nothing look cooler or seem more appealing than being young and in love and living carefree in a wooden shack on the beach in Languedoc.

It's only after their shack burns down and they move to Paris that things begin to go wrong for the characters Betty and Zorg, and they find out the true meaning of *l'amour fou*.

©SIR FRANCIS CANKER PHOTOGRAPHY/GETTY IMAGES

In Bruges

2008

Relais Bourgondisch Cruyce hotel, Bruges, Belgium

In Martin McDonagh's spiky black comedy, two Irish hitmen are sent to lie low in Bruges, and are booked into this historic timbered canalside hotel. One hitman is understandably delighted with the opportunity to get to see what he has heard is 'the best-preserved medieval city in the whole of Belgium'; the other follows in tow like a sulky teenager. 'If I grew up on a farm, and was retarded, Bruges might impress me,' he says. 'But I didn't so it doesn't.'

There's no accounting for taste.

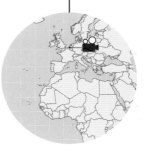

©PETER HARRISON/GETTY IMAGES

Muriel's Wedding

1994

Hamilton Island, Queensland, Australia

Are you an ugly duckling living a dowdy life in Porpoise Spit, provincial Australia? Well why not leave it behind and come to Hibiscus Island. (Or Hamilton Island, as it's called in the real world.) More than just an idyllic honeymoon resort, it's the sort of place that can change your life, where you can finally face your Waterloo, and where your romantic fantasies will finally begin to come true.

©VICTOR MASCHEK/SHUTTERSTOCK

Thelma & Louise

1991

Dead Horse Point State Park, Utah, USA

Despite what is suggested on screen, it actually isn't the Grand Canyon that Thelma and Louise speed Louise's Thunderbird into at the end of their feminist buddy road movie, but rather the ravine carved by the Colorado River in Utah's Canyonlands. But as a gesture and a statement, it's still pretty grand. As is the canyon, for that matter.

©VALESTOCK/SHUTTERSTOCK.COM

Seinfeld

1989–98

Tom's Restaurant, New York, USA

It might look like just another unassuming New York diner on Broadway, but this is the place where George Costanza was inspired to become his opposite, where Jerry worked out the semiotics of pie sharing, and where four friends devised a contest that would test their mastery of their domains.

It's a bit like how Seinfeld was supposed to be a show about nothing, but turned out to be one of the great philosophical texts of our time.

When Harry Met Sally

1989

Katz's Delicatessen, New York, USA

The characters in films including *Donnie Brasco*, and *Enchanted* all ate there too, but Katz's Delicatessen on Manhattan's Lower East Side, est. 1888, will always be Harry and Sally's place. How often do you think the staff are asked if a patron can 'have what she's having'? The current owner has stopped counting, but does say that someone fakes an orgasm there at least once a day.

©GARY LATHAM/LONELY PLANET

Crouching Tiger, Hidden Dragon

2000

Anji County bamboo forest, Zhejiang Province, China

It takes a lifetime of kung fu training to be able to gracefully balance on the swaying tops of 30m tall bamboo plants, or have a sword fight up there. But the 40-hectare Zhong Guo da Zhu Hai forest – literally: China Big Bamboo Sea – looks pretty stunning at ground level, too.

©IMAGEMORE CO.,LTD./GETTY IMAGES

Batman Begins

2005

St Pancras Chambers, London, UK

The central staircase in the grand gothic revival hotel designed by Sir Gilbert Scott in 1873, and attached to St Pancras station, was used for scenes in *Batman Begins* in which the Scarecrow lets loose a hallucinogenic drug in Arkham Asylum.

It wasn't the first time the staircase was witness to lunatics taking over the asylum. The Spice Girls danced on it in the video for their debut single 'Wannabe'.

Out of Africa

1985

Maasai Mara, Kenya

'There's country there you ought to see,' says big-game hunter Denys Finch Hatton (Robert Redford) to plantation owner Karen Blixen (Meryl Streep) in the romantic epic *Out of Africa*. But it's a film in which what is now Kenya, but they knew as British East Africa, takes a semi-mystical hold over its characters – so if you don't want to risk it, the Oscar-winning cinematography by David Watkin is the next best thing.

Harry Potter and the Philosopher's Stone

2001
Australia House, the Strand, London

This suitably stately and imposing building is the home of Gringotts Wizarding Bank, est. 1417: one of the oldest, most reputable and most-liked financial institutions in existence, and 'the safest place in the world for anything you want to keep safe'. Pity the poor muggles whose bankers aren't goblins.

©CHRISDORNEY/GETTY IMAGES

©KERIN FORSTMANIS/ALAMY STOCK PHOTO

Picnic at Hanging Rock

1975

Hanging Rock, Victoria, Australia

Australian cinema, perhaps to a greater extent than any other national cinema, is obsessed with the country's landscape. It's no surprise, then, that its first breakout international hit derives so much of its eerie, mesmeric power from an unusual 6.25 million-year-old geological formation known as a mamelon.

©NAEBLYS/ALAMY STOCK PHOTO

The Birds

1963

The Potter Schoolhouse, Bodega, California, USA

The 19th-century redwood schoolhouse that features in the most chilling scene in Alfred Hitchcock's late masterpiece – the one which begins with the birds slowly but unmistakably and ominously gathering on the children's climbing frame – doesn't appear in Daphne du Maurier's source novella. Mind you, if Hitch had followed the book more closely the film would have been set in Cornwall instead of coastal California and Tippi Hedren would have needed to adopt a West Country burr.

© PAUL HAWTHORNE / STAFF/GETTY IMAGES

The Amityville Horror

1979

112 Ocean Avenue, Amityville, New York, USA

In 1974, the house at 112 Ocean Avenue in Amityville, New York, became the scene of a notorious multiple domestic murder, when a 23-year-old man killed the other six members of his family who lived there. But the house was not, contrary to the claims made in a number of books and films, built on an ancient Native American burial ground. And nor was it haunted.

What a boon to the films' producers and poster artists, though, that the attic windows could be made to give the house such a malevolent look.

©KEVIN KOZICKI/GETTY IMAGES

The Princess Bride

1987

The Cliffs of Moher, Ireland

Facing the Atlantic from the southwest of Ireland, the Cliffs of Moher are 8km long, 213m high and ruffled like piped icing. You can see why they might cause any Sicilian scoundrels who come sailing by in a postmodern fairytale to exclaim that they have spied: 'the Cliffs of Insanity!'

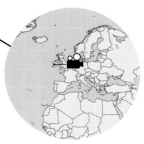

©DAN WELLDON/LONELY PLANET

Ferris Bueller's Day Off

1986

**Art Institute
of Chicago**

Ferris Bueller: 1980s teen movie icon, tech wizard, truant, art lover. He may strike some people as a little smug, but there's absolutely no arguing with his personal motto: 'Life moves pretty fast. If you don't stop and look around once in a while, you could miss it.'

The painting shown here, which so entrances his friend Cameron, is *A Sunday Afternoon on the Island of La Grande Jatte* (1884), George Seurat's pointillist portrait of Parisians at leisure.

©SAM DIEPHUIS/GETTY IMAGES

The Harder They Come

1972

Kingston, Jamaica

Some films can really put a place on the map. Others can change the whole culture.

Crime drama *The Harder They Come*, starring Jimmy Cliff as a young man who moves to the city in search of his fortune, was Jamaica's first indigenous feature film and introduced the wider world to Jamaican patois, Kingston slum-life, Rastafari culture and – above all – reggae music.

©MARKUS ULRICH/500PX

The Secret Life of Walter Mitty

2013
Kirkjufell, Snæfellsnes, Iceland

Ben Stiller's reworking of the James Thurber story *The Secret Life of Walter Mitty* makes it a parable about the imperative to throw off the shackles of the everyday and travel, have adventures and seize the day. Seeing Mitty skateboard down Kirkjufell mountain in Iceland, one is inclined to agree.

©MARK ZUKOWSKI/500PX

Indiana Jones and the Kingdom of the Crystal Skull

2008

Ghost Ranch, New Mexico, USA

The US Air Force facility Area 51 plays a significant part in Dr Jones's fourth big adventure. But the US Air Force is famously protective of the secrecy surrounding that particular base, which is probably why the production got this spectacular bit of the New Mexico landscape (which was also home to and inspiration for the painter Georgia O'Keeffe) to stand in for Nevada in the opening chase sequence.

©CHANCE HAMMOCK/500PX

Forrest Gump

1994

**Lincoln Memorial,
Washington DC, USA**

As one of America's most symbolic sites – where the country's most cherished ideals are venerated, and where the 250,000-strong March on Washington heard Martin Luther King describe his dream – the Lincoln Memorial has made an appearance in many movies. *Mr Smith Goes to Washington* and *The Day the Earth Stood Still*, for example. As well as the scene in the heartwarming revisionist account of US history, *Forrest Gump*, in which Gump is reunited with his lost love at an anti–Vietnam War rally.

Rebel Without a Cause

1955

Griffith Observatory, Los Angeles, California, USA

The best place to see the stars in LA – along with the Ivy, the Chateau Marmont and the Walk of Fame – has featured in dozens of films. Notably, it's where Arnie's T-800 first shows up in 1984 in *The Terminator*. But the observatory is most indelibly linked with James Dean, whose troubled character Jim Stark goes there on a school trip, gets challenged to a game of chicken, and pretty much defines teenage cool.

©PHOTOGRAPH BY ASIM BHARWANI/GETTY IMAGES/MOMENT RF

Ran

1985

Himeji Castle, Kansai, Japan

In Akira Kurosawa's late masterpiece *Ran* – an extraordinary version of King Lear and Japan's most expensive film at the time – an ageing warlord gives away what is sometimes called 'White Heron Castle', and almost immediately comes to regret doing so.

You can see why. The beautiful, early Edo-period, 83-building complex would have been the very latest in castle design at the time. And it remains the county's most storied, most visited, best preserved castle; a World Heritage Site and officially designated National Treasure.

©STEVEN DUNCAN/500PX

©LEONID SEREBRENNIKOV/ALAMY STOCK PHOTO

Die Hard

1988

Fox Plaza, Century City, Los Angeles, USA

Sometimes, to paraphrase The Wizard of Oz, you find what you've been searching for was at home all along. Sometimes, location scouts are just lazy.

The building that became Nakatomi Plaza and has a starring role in the daddy of all hostage movies is Fox Plaza in Century City, LA – the headquarters of the studio that made the film, 20th Century Fox.

©BGSMITH/SHUTTERSTOCK

The Revenant

2015
Kananaskis, Alberta, Canada

Look at this fabulous wilderness. It's beautiful, yes, but can you imagine trying to eke out an existence there? Freezing temperatures, food shortages, the threat of molestation by bear... and that's just for the cast and crew of Alejandro González Iñárritu's Oscar-winning survival thriller. For the early 19th-century Midwestern fur trappers and frontierspeople on whose lives the film is based, conditions were even worse.

©MARK BASSETT/ALAMY STOCK PHOTO

Lost in Translation

2003

Park Hyatt Hotel, Shinjuku, Tokyo, Japan

If Sofia Coppola's wistful almost-romance *Lost in Translation* is to be believed, then even amid the high-end luxury of a hotel such as the Park Hyatt – occupying the top 14 floors of a glass skyscraper by Kenzo Tange in Tokyo's Shinjuku district – it is possible to feel disconnected, jaded and unloved.

It's nothing that can't be improved by meeting a fellow weary traveller, leaving the hotel, seeing the city and singing karaoke, however.

©JOHN FREEMAN/GETTY IMAGES

Once

2007

**Grafton Street,
Dublin, Ireland**

John Carney's wistful naturalistic musical, which is about the brief romance between a busker and the young Czech woman who approaches him in Grafton Street one day, was made for not much more than the coins in a busker's hat, and went on to win hearts and awards all around the world. Thus proving that the streets of Dublin really are paved with dreams.

©CHRISTIAN BERTRAND/GETTY IMAGES

Amélie

2001

Café des 2 Moulins, Montmartre, Paris, France

Amélie Poulain, doer of good deeds, skimmer of stones and Madonna of the unloved, works as a waitress at the Café des 2 Moulins in Montmartre. It's a real place, sat halfway between the Moulin Rouge and the Moulin de la Galette, the two windmills turned cabarets from which it takes its name.

Just don't expect it it look exactly the same when you go: *Amélie* is a paean to those – like its heroine and also, you suspect, its director – who see the world a little differently to everyone else.

©BAMBOOME/GETTY IMAGES

The Assassin

2015

Wudang Mountains, Hubei, China

History and legend intertwine up on the Wudang Mountains, where a complex of 62 surviving palaces, temples, monasteries and shrines is carved into the rock. A centre for Taoism in the 7th century, it is also said to be the birthplace of the fabled Wu-Tang Clan, regular stars of the *wuxia* tradition of Chinese martial arts cinema.

It isn't an easy place to take a film crew, but you can see the complex in *Crouching Tiger, Hidden Dragon*, and the Taiwanese director Hou Hsiao-Hsien's exquisite 2015 arthouse *wuxia The Assassin*.

Vertigo

1958

San Francisco Bay, California, USA

Having been tailed all over the city for the day, disturbed Hitchcock blonde Madeleine Elster (or is it Carlotta? Or Judy?) jumps from outside Fort Point, under the shadow of the Golden Gate Bridge, into San Francisco Bay. It's possible to retrace her steps, but beware getting caught in a kind of endless return of regret and romantic obsession.

©ANDREW MONTGOMERY/LONELY PLANET

©JOHNER IMAGES/GETTY IMAGES

The Bridge

2011-

Øresund Bridge, between Sweden and Denmark

It's difficult to say whether the huge global popularity of Nordic noir – with all its moral complexities and murders, glum characters and gloomy weather, knitted brows and knitted jumpers – has been good or bad for Scandinavia's image and tourist trade. Take the 12km bridge that spans the Øresund Strait: a remarkable engineering feat, completed in 2000, expressly designed as a symbol of co-operation, now indelibly linked with the fiendish machinations of a fictional serial killer.

©MEANMACHINE77/SHUTTERSTOCK

Planet of the Apes

1968

**Westward Beach,
Point Dume, Malibu,
California, USA**

Tied in first place with the final shot of *The 400 Blows,* the ending (spoiler alert!) of *Planet of the Apes* – featuring Charlton Heston, Linda Harrison and Lady Liberty – is the joint most famous closing beach scene in movie history.

It's also one of the only times in cinema that a Malibu exterior was used for New York.

©FRANK CHMURA/GETTY IMAGES

The Talented
Mr Ripley

1999

Ischia, Gulf of Naples, Italy

With its pastel-washed fishing villages reflecting in the azure waters of the Bay of Naples like some unspoiled, lesser known Portofino, the island of Ischia looks like just the sort of place the international idle rich of the 1960s might have picked as a playground in which to loll around in cream linen suits and Wayfarers, smoke, listen to jazz and contemplate life. Or identity theft and murder.

©DENNIS K. JOHNSON/GETTY IMAGES

Monty Python and the Holy Grail

1975

Doune Castle, Stirling, Scotland

Built in the 13th century, then remodelled in the late 14th by the Duke of Albany, Doune Castle is fairly typical of medieval strongholds of the time, with a 30m gatehouse containing the lord's domestic quarters and two guardrooms, and ramparts from which to lob cows and dadaist, outrageously French-accented insults at any Arthurian knights who should happen to come clippity-clopping by. Example: 'Your mother was a hamster and your father smelt of elderberries.'

©CREATIVENATUREMEDIA/GETTY IMAGES

The Wicker Man

1973

Burrow Head, Scotland

Look at the fearsome stark beauty of this bit of land. Doesn't it make you want to worship the ancient pagan gods who are surely responsible? Placate them with the occasional human sacrifice, perhaps? At the very least, it looks like a good place for some maypole dancing.

Actually, Burrow Head is on the Scottish mainland and not the Hebrides where the 1973 folk-horror movie is set, but the point still stands. As, until recently, did the charred stumps of the wicker man prop.

©NICK FOX/SHUTTERSTOCK

Harry Potter and the Philosopher's Stone

2001

Glenfinnan Viaduct, Inverness-shire, Scotland

Snaking for 257km, the West Highland Line is one of the world's most scenic railways. And with its 21 arches, each 30m high and with a 15m span, the Glenfinnan Viaduct at the top of Loch Shiel is one of its most impressive bridges. And at the beginning of every school term, a magic locomotive crosses the viaduct during its non-stop journey from King's Cross in London to Hogwarts School of Witchcraft and Wizardry.

©HEMIS/ALAMY STOCK PHOTO

Midnight in Paris

2011

Le Polidor, Paris, France

The Polidor is a Parisian Left Bank institution that has remained largely unchanged for more than a century and a half, and serves the same traditional French cuisine that it always has. If you dine there today, you may fancy that you can still feel something of the presence of the literary and artistic giants who were regulars in the past – Victor Hugo, Arthur Rimbaud, Ernest Hemingway, James Joyce, Henry Miller. Or, if you're in a Woody Allen fantasy, you may meet some of them for real.

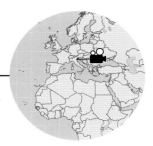

©PIERE BONBON/ALAMY STOCK PHOTO

Don't Look Now

1973

San Nicolò dei Mendicoli, Venice, Italy

The eternal city never seemed more mysterious or more haunted than in Nicolas Roeg's extraordinary Daphne du Maurier adaptation about a grieving couple. The ornate interiors that Donald Sutherland's character is restoring belong to the 12th-century church of San Nicolò dei Mendicoli. The small figure in the red anorak is not who she seems.

Close Encounters of the Third Kind

1977

Devils Tower, Wyoming, USA

The second most famous monolith in science fiction cinema is a geologically extraordinary 265m-tall protrusion of igneous rock that doubles as a perfect UFO landing site. In 1906, President Roosevelt designated it America's first National Monument, and it receives 400,000 visitors annually. It you don't get to be one of them, you can always do like Richard Dreyfus and make your own out of mashed potato.

©MARK READ/LONELY PLANET

©EWG3D/GETTY IMAGES

The Pianist

2002

Praga, Warsaw, Poland

The Warsaw ghetto to which the pianist Władysław Szpilman was confined in 1940 was razed in 1943, and over time the area was entirely rebuilt. So Roman Polanski shot his Oscar-winning film about Szpilman in Praga, a relatively untouched – even derelict – city district that had faced the ghetto from the other side of the river.

Praga is now where all the city's artists and hipsters live, but, in some part thanks to films such as *The Pianist*, the past is not forgotten.

©KIEV.VICTOR/SHUTTERSTOCK

Four Weddings and a Funeral

1994

Old Royal Naval College Greenwich, London, UK

There must be something quintessentially English about Sir Christopher Wren's 18th-century Royal Naval College (formerly Greenwich Hospital). It doubled for Buckingham Palace in *The King's Speech*, *The Iron Lady* and *The Queen*, while it has played stately homes in *Sense and Sensibility*, *The Wings of the Dove* and *The Duchess*.

It's no wonder that the poshest of the weddings in that charming ode to posh *Englishness*, *Four Weddings and a Funeral*, was held in the building's chapel and grounds.

Star Wars: The Force Awakens

2015

Skellig Michael, County Kerry, Ireland

This isolated 6th-century monastery was pretty much the furthermost outpost of what remained of Western civilisation throughout the dark ages. George Bernard Shaw described it as an 'incredible, impossible, mad place', adding that it 'does not belong to any world that you and I have lived and worked in: it is part of our dream world.'

Indeed, a long time ago in some far, far away galaxy, it was the first Jedi temple.

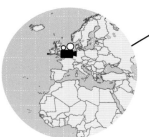

CHRIS WAHLBERG/GETTY IMAGES ©

©JOE WINDSOR-WILLIAMS/LONELY PLANET

The Battle of Algiers

1966

Casbah of Algiers, Algeria

When a film-maker strives for realism, or the truth, location decisions are often made for him.

One of the original docu-dramas, Gillo Pontecorvo's shockingly, heart-racingly contemporary film was made less than a decade after Algiers' Casbah was rocked by the guerrilla warfare waged by Algeria's National Liberation Front against the occupying French forces. It was shot on black and white newsreel film, in the same streets that witnessed the fighting and still bore the scars.

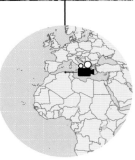

©SIMON CROCKETT/GETTY IMAGES

Broadchurch

2013–

West Bay, Dorset, UK

In this gripping British TV drama, the body of an 11-year-old boy is discovered on this stretch of Dorset's Jurassic Coast, and the investigation into his death reveals the outwardly idyllic small town of Broadchurch as a hotbed of iniquity and suspicious behaviour.

It's not all child murder and gloom in that part of the British televisual landscape, however, as it's just a pebble's throw from where Keith and Candice-Marie go camping in Mike Leigh's 1976 TV play and comic masterpiece *Nuts in May*.

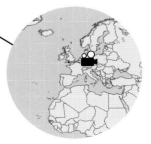

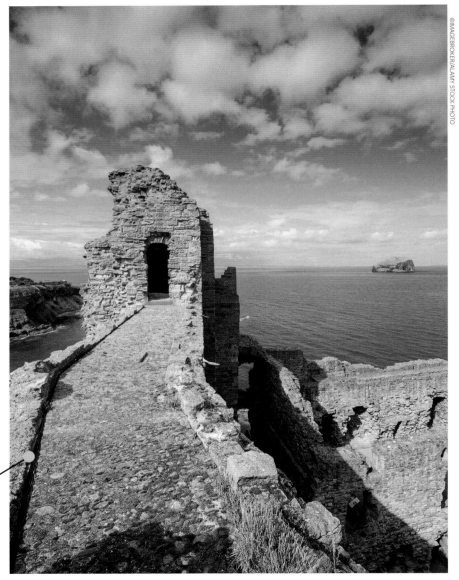

©IMAGEBROKER/ALAMY STOCK PHOTO

Under the Skin

2014

Tantallon Castle, East Lothian, Scotland

One of the simplest but most powerful effects in Jonathan Glazer's alien-predator drama was achieved by shooting with hidden cameras, guerilla-style, on ordinary streets in Glasgow's town centre, where, with the greatest respect to the people of Glasgow, Scarlett Johansson's beauty makes her nameless character stand out and seem otherworldly.

Scotland gets to show off its own fearsome beauty later in the film though, when the alien heads into the Highlands, visits the ruins of this 14th-century castle, and seems to admit a sliver of light into its soul.

©JUAN GABALDON/500PX

Fitzcarraldo

1982
Iquitos, Peru

Iquitos, sometimes called the capital of the Peruvian Amazon, is the largest city in the world that is inaccessible by road. You can get there by air or river easily enough if you'd like to visit. Or on foot through the jungle if you're adventurous.

Just don't try dragging a 300-tonne steamship along with you. As attested by Werner Herzog's film *Fitzcarraldo* – and even more so by the making-of documentary *Burden of Dreams* – that requires a special kind of wild, mad, quixotic obsession.

©GIONNIXXX/GETTY IMAGES

Apocalypse Now

1979

Pagsanjan, Laguna, Luzon, Philippines

The difficulties involved in shooting *Apocalypse Now* in the Philippines famously included – but were not limited to – the director's nervous breakdown, the leading man's heart attack, the personal eccentricities of Marlon Brando, various tropical diseases, the Filipino army having to ask for its helicopters back to fight an insurgency, and the destruction of all the sets by typhoon Olga.

But would it have been the mad masterpiece it is if it were made anywhere else?

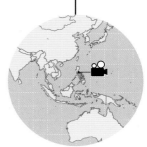

©MICHAEL MATTHEWS/ALAMY STOCK PHOTO

The Breakfast Club

1985

Maine North High School, Des Plaines, Illinois, USA

This nondescript municipal building, which now houses a police headquarters and the regional offices of various bureaucratic state agencies, might not look like much. And perhaps it isn't.

But for the duration of one Saturday in 1985, it was home to a rebel, a geek, a jock, a prom queen and a misfit who deconstructed and redefined teen movie archetypes forever.

©NATIONAL GEOGRAPHIC CREATIVE/ALAMY STOCK PHOTO

Dr No

1962

Oracabessa, St Mary, Jamaica

For audiences in the era before affordable air travel, the globetrotting required of 007 in the performance of his duties contributed more to the glamour and appeal of the James Bond films than anything else.

But the series began close to his home, in the Jamaican bay where Ian Fleming built his Goldeneye estate and wrote all the 007 books, where Sean Connery has a go at singing calypso, and where Ursula Andress emerges from the sea to create one of the most iconic images in Sixties cinema.

©JAARON MORGAN/500PX

Stand By Me

1986

Lake Britton railway bridge, Shasta County, California, USA

For the kids in *Stand By Me*, hastily crossing this trestle bridge becomes one of the most memorable parts of their rite of passage. But that doesn't mean it was advisable. Far from it. Re-enacting the scene probably isn't advisable either, but the line has been abandoned and the track removed so at least you aren't going to be hit by a train.

Blade Runner

1982

Bradbury Building, Los Angeles, USA

Ridley Scott is one of the film's great visual stylists. His 1982 film *Blade Runner* continues to look more like the future than almost any other sci-fi film. And with judicious use of noirish mood lighting, he was able to make the gorgeous art deco Bradbury building, one of LA's architectural wonders, look like the sort of place you'd only live if there was no new life awaiting you in the off-world colonies.

©LAURENCE PHELAN

Battleship Potemkin

1925

Odessa Steps, Odessa, Ukraine

Much of the grammar of action cinema was invented here, in the sequence in which jackboots advance down the steps leading from the city of Odessa to the seafront, the Cossack army opens fire on the unarmed townspeople, and a pram goes careening towards the bottom.

Hitchcock paid homage to the scene in *Foreign Correspondent*, as did Woody Allen in *Bananas*, Terry Gilliam in *Brazil* and Brian De Palma in *The Untouchables*.

©IPPL/SHUTTERSTOCK.COM

Film & TV Locations: a Spotter's Guide

April 2017
Published by Lonely Planet Global Limited
CRN 554153
www.lonelyplanet.com
2 3 4 5 6 7 8 9 10
Printed in Singapore
ISBN 978 1786 57760 3
© Lonely Planet 2016
© photographers as indicated 2016

Written by Laurence Phelan

Managing Director, Publishing Piers Pickard
Associate Publisher & Commissioning Editor Robin Barton
Art Director Daniel Di Paolo
Layout Designer Lauren Egan
Editor Ross Taylor
Print Production Larissa Frost, Nigel Longuet

All rights reserved. No part of this publication may be reproduced, stored in a retrieval system or transmitted in any form by any means, electronic, mechanical, photocopying, recording or otherwise except brief extracts for the purpose of review, without the written permission of the publisher. Lonely Planet and the Lonely Planet logo are trademarks of Lonely Planet and are registered in the US patent and Trademark Office and in other countries.

Lonely Planet Offices

Australia
The Malt Store, Level 3, 551 Swanston St, Carlton, Victoria 3053
T: 03 8379 8000

Ireland
Unit E, Digital Court, The Digital Hub, Rainsford St, Dublin 8

USA
124 Linden St, Oakland, CA 94607 T: 510 250 6400

UK
240 Blackfriars Rd, London SE1 8NW T: 020 3771 5100

STAY IN TOUCH lonelyplanet.com/contact

Although the authors and Lonely Planet have taken all reasonable care in preparing this book, we make no warranty about the accuracy or completeness of its content and, to the maximum extent permitted, disclaim all liability from its use.

COVER IMAGES CLOCKWISE FROM TOP LEFT:
© NICK FOX/SHUTTERSTOCK,© VISTAS©RAKESHSONI/GETTIYIMAGES,
© JOE WINDSOR-WILLIAMS/LONELY PLANET,© JUSTIN FOULKES/
LONLEY PLANET, © DAN HUNTLEY/GETTYIMAGES, © ALYAKSANDR
STZHALKOUSKI/500PX, © STEVEN DUNCAN/SHUTTERSTOCK

Paper in this book is certified against the Forest Stewardship Council™ standards. FSC™ promotes environmentally responsible, socially beneficial and economically viable management of the world's forests.